W9-BLR-517

COOL
Science Projects
with
Technology

Electric
MOTOR
Experiments

Ed Sobey, Ph. D.

Enslow Publishers, Inc.
40 Industrial Road
Box 398
Berkeley Heights, NJ 07922
USA

http://www.enslow.com

To the Geoduck Express—197 miles running
and still going strong

Acknowledgments:

Thanks to Susan Johnson and Bellevue Community College for one of the photos that appears in this book. I also thank all the kids over the years who have been so excited to build models with electric motors. Your enthusiasm and creativity inspire me.

Library of Congress Cataloging-in-Publication Data

Sobey, Edwin J. C., 1948–
    Electric motor experiments / Ed Sobey.
        p. cm. — (Cool science projects with technology)
    Includes bibliographical references and index.
    Summary: "Presents several science projects dealing with electric motors"—
        Provided by publisher.
    ISBN 978-0-7660-3306-1
    1. Electric motors—Juvenile literature. 2. Science projects—Juvenile literature.
    I. Title.
    TK9911.S63 2011
    621.46078—dc22

                                                        2009037895

Printed in the United States of America

122010 Lake Book Manufacturing, Inc., Melrose Park, IL

10 9 8 7 6 5 4 3 2 1

To Our Readers: We have done our best to make sure all Internet Addresses in this book were active and appropriate when we went to press. However, the author and the publisher have no control over and assume no liability for the material available on those Internet sites or on other Web sites they may link to. Any comments or suggestions can be sent by e-mail to comments@enslow.com or to the address on the back cover.

♻ Enslow Publishers, Inc., is committed to printing our books on recycled paper. The paper in every book contains 10% to 30% post-consumer waste (PCW). The cover board on the outside of each book contains 100% PCW. Our goal is to do our part to help young people and the environment too!

Photo Credits: All photos by Ed Sobey, except Susan Johnson, p. 83; Shutterstock.com, p. 77.

Cover Photo: © iStockPhoto.com (teen); Ed Sobey (vehicle)

Contents

Experiments with a 🏅 symbol feature Ideas for Your Science Fair.

Experiments with a ✸ symbol feature Ideas for Your Science Fair.

Motors—Making Things Move

Think of all the machines you see that move or move things. Elevators and escalators, automatic doors, some movie screens that move up and down, fans, and computer printers are a few examples. At home, you might have a washer and dryer, blender, or electric toothbrush. All these machines have motors, and most are powered by electricity.

If you want to build something that moves, you will probably need at least one electric motor. This book will show you how to create gizmos that move. Once you understand the basics, you can design and build an endless number of motorized models.

The magic of motors starts when you connect them to a power source. All of the experiments in this book use batteries for power. **Do not use any motors that require you to plug them into a wall outlet.** Batteries provide plenty of power for the models, and they are safe to use.

Connecting a battery to a motor with two wires rewards you with the high-speed whir of the fast-spinning motor shaft. The whir confirms that energy is flowing from the battery to make the motor spin.

Besides initiating a series of reactions, making the simple connection between the battery and motor also

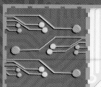

launches you on a quest to find inventive ways to control that connection and to use the output mechanical force. You can make simple switches with stuff you have at school or home to open and complete the circuit. Then you can make a variety of gizmos that you power with electric motors.

Besides reading this book, the best way to learn about electric motors is to experiment with them. Get an inexpensive motor from an electronics or hobby store, science catalog, or school. You can also find motors in old computer equipment and other electronics that people have thrown away. You might find several motors to use inside an old CD player or VCR. Then gather batteries, battery holders, and alligator clip leads for connectors. Ask lots of questions and conduct experiments to find the answers. In your experiments, **do not connect anything to an electrical outlet in your home or school and do not directly connect the positive and negative terminals of a battery.** Directly connecting the positive and negative battery terminals makes a short circuit (see Figure 1.1) and will quickly ruin your battery.

The Scientific Method

You can run many great experiments with motors, but to use these in a scientific report or science fair, you need to follow a few guidelines. Conducting a scientific experiment includes making observations, measuring variables, collecting and analyzing data, researching scientific articles, and producing an attractive and easy-to-understand report. Simply making a machine that uses motors isn't science.

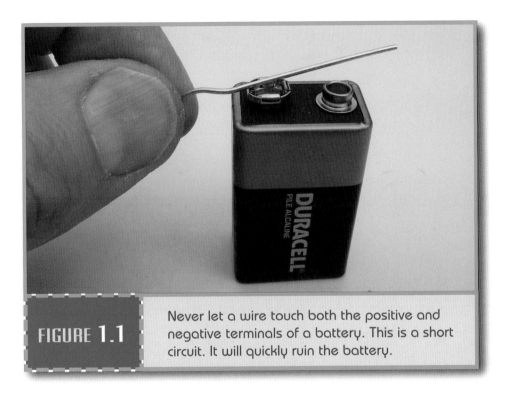

| FIGURE 1.1 | Never let a wire touch both the positive and negative terminals of a battery. This is a short circuit. It will quickly ruin the battery. |

Start your project by experimenting with motors. Ask yourself questions about how they operate and what they can do. As you learn more, ask better and more detailed questions. Before running an experiment, think of a possible answer, or hypothesis. The experiment can test whether your hypothesis is true or false.

A good question is one that you can answer by running a test and collecting data (numbers). Being able to represent that data in a graph helps people understand what you have discovered. As you conduct experiments, remember to change

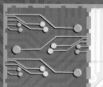

only one variable at a time. If you change more than one variable at once, you won't be able to tell which one caused the effects you see.

You could experiment with different ways to get the motor's motion to power wheels or other parts. If you want to make electric car models, you could power the car with a propeller attached to the motor shaft, or you could attach a wheel directly to the motor shaft. Other options would be to use gears or a belt (such as a rubber band) on the motor shaft to spin the wheels or axles. Each design will operate differently. You could measure how fast each model travels or how much weight each model can pull. As you experiment, you will come up with new ideas to try.

Your first job is to get a notebook in which you can record information about each experiment you conduct. Each entry should have a date so that you can keep track of when you did each experiment. List the materials you use, and keep notes on what you try and what results you observe. Add sketches of designs and circuits that you use. Add photos if you can. You will be able to build on these notes for a long, long time.

Remember the first two rules of science. Rule number one is to stop doing what you are doing whenever you find something interesting. Go explore the interesting thing and see where it leads. Rule number two: Have fun. Science is a fun process of discovery and learning.

Safety First

The projects included in this book are perfectly safe. However, read these safety rules before you start any project.

1. All of the experiments in this book use batteries for power. Do not use any motors that require you to plug them into a wall outlet.

2. Do any experiments or projects, whether from this book or of your own design, under the supervision of a science teacher or other knowledgeable adult.

3. Read all instructions carefully before proceeding with a project. If you have questions, check with your supervisor before going any further.

4. Maintain a serious attitude while conducting experiments. Fooling around can be dangerous to you and to others.

5. Wear approved safety goggles when you are doing anything that might cause injury to your eyes.

6. Have a first-aid kit nearby while you are experimenting.

7. Do not eat or drink while experimenting.

8. Always wear shoes, not sandals, while experimenting.

The Shocking Truth About Electricity

E ven though electricity was discovered centuries ago, we are still discovering new things that it can do. Making things move by using electric motors is one of the most common uses of electricity. If you take apart a toy that moves, for example a radio-controlled (RC) car, you will find two motors. One drives the car forward and the other provides steering. These motors, like most motors used in toys, operate with the power from one or several batteries. Any battery that is shaped like a cylinder delivers 1.5 volts, regardless of how large (D cell) or small (AAA cell) the battery is. Connecting two batteries together so that the positive end of one connects to the negative end of the other will double the voltage. This arrangement of batteries is called a series circuit (see Figure 2.1). In series circuits, the total voltage is the voltage of each battery added together. An RC car typically has four batteries connected in series to deliver 6 volts (1.5 volts per battery).

For a motor to spin, it has to be connected to a battery. If you look at a battery, you will see that it has two ends, or terminals. One is marked + and one is marked −. Looking at a motor will show that it also has two terminals, or places to make a connection. However, these terminals aren't marked + and –. For the motor to operate, wires need to be connected from one battery terminal to one motor terminal and from the second battery terminal to the second motor terminal. This is called a complete circuit. When experimenting with motors, you will find that they spin faster when the voltage applied to them is higher. The higher voltage

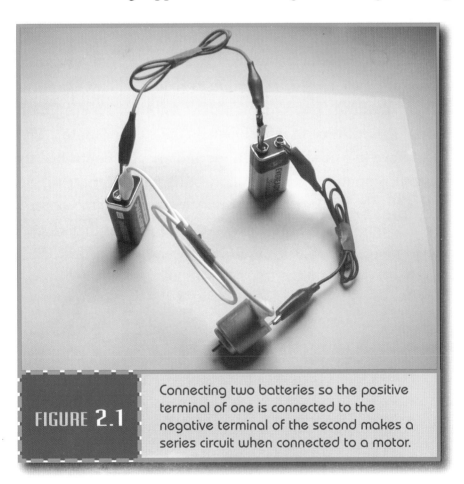

FIGURE 2.1

Connecting two batteries so the positive terminal of one is connected to the negative terminal of the second makes a series circuit when connected to a motor.

pushes more energy into the motor and makes it spin faster. However, each motor is made to operate within a certain range of voltages. If you keep adding batteries in series, you will exceed the motor's range and it will break. If the motor needs more voltage than the battery is supplying, it won't spin even though the circuit is complete. If the circuit isn't complete, the motor will not spin.

As you explore motors, you will find that some of them have more than two terminals. Motors with three terminals are servo motors. These are used in robots and other machines where precise motion is required. You cannot use them without a microcomputer. Another type of motor that delivers precise movements is the stepper motor. These can have five or six connections and are also controlled by a microcomputer. There are many other types of motors. Some do not spin, but instead move back and forth. In this book, we will use the simple direct current (DC) motors that spin, use low voltage from a battery, and are inexpensive to buy.

How Many Motors Do You Have at Home?

1. Take a guess as to how many motors you will find in your home. Then begin your search. Be sure to record what you find in your experiment notebook.

2. Start by looking in the kitchen. How many machines there move things? Mixers, blenders, coffee grinders, and electric knives are a few of the things you might find. How about the refrigerator? It has a compressor that is driven by an electric motor, and it might also have an ice maker that has a motor. Is there a fan in the kitchen?

3. If your family has a computer, check that out next. What machines connected to the computer or in the computer cause things to move or spin?

4. Look for a VCR or DVD player and other entertainment devices.

5. If you have a garage, how do the doors open? Are there electric tools there or in the basement?

Things you will need

- pencil
- notebook

13

You won't get shocked doing experiments from this book. This is because all of the experiments use batteries, not alternating current from a wall outlet. Batteries supply electricity at a much lower voltage and are safe to use.

Many modern devices run on batteries. This allows you to use them anywhere, as long as you can either recharge or replace the batteries. When you purchase batteries, you look for batteries that will fit the device you want to power. Do you also look at the label on the side of batteries? What voltage do the batteries deliver?

Most common batteries are AAA, AA, C, D, lantern, and transistor or 9 volt. If you have some of these, take a look at them. What is the voltage on AAA, AA, C, or D batteries? These cylindrical batteries all provide 1.5 volts. A lantern battery provides 6 volts and a transistor battery provides 9 volts.

It might seem odd that all four of the most common batteries provide the same voltage: 1.5 volts. The chemical reaction inside each of these batteries converts chemical energy into the same amount of electricity, regardless of the battery's size. No matter how large you make that battery it provides 1.5 volts because that's all the electricity that can come from that type of chemical reaction.

The larger the battery, the longer it can provide the 1.5 volts to power your appliance or toy. A D battery will outlast a double A (AA) battery, because a D battery has almost ten times as much energy as a double A (AA).

If the chemical reaction of a battery produces 1.5 volts, how are 6-volt lantern batteries and 9-volt transistor batteries made? Note that the voltages of each of these is a whole number multiple of 1.5 volts. Inside a 6-volt lantern battery there are 4 smaller batteries that each produces 1.5 volts. These batteries are arranged in a series circuit. A series of batteries is one in which the positive terminal of one battery is connected to the negative terminal of the next battery. In series, the voltages add up, so having four batteries that each produces 1.5 volts gives a lantern battery an output of 6 volts. The transistor battery has six smaller batteries inside, giving 6 times 1.5 volts, or 9 volts. The other way to connect batteries is in a parallel circuit (Figure 2.2).

Batteries are an expensive way to provide electric power. If you are going to do lots of experiments with motors consider buying rechargeable batteries and a charger for them.

FIGURE 2.2

Connecting two batteries so both positive terminals are connected and both negative terminals are connected makes a parallel circuit when connected to a motor.

6. You might find electric motors even in the bathroom. Some people have electric toothbrushes, electric razors, and hair dryers.

7. After you have checked every room in the house and recorded all the motors you found, see how the total number compares to your initial guess. Did you find a lot more motors that you thought you had?

Open a Transistor Battery

Few people look inside batteries because most expect batteries to contain dangerous chemicals. In this experiment, you won't touch any corrosive chemicals. The one danger to watch out for is poking yourself with a screwdriver when you try to open the battery.

1. What do you expect to find inside a 9-volt battery? Many people answer "acid" because common batteries once used acid. However, it is more likely that the battery in your hand doesn't have acid inside. The chemical it uses is potassium hydroxide, which is not an acid. You still want to avoid the chemical, but it is not acidic. Follow these steps so that you don't touch the chemical.

Things you will need

- discarded 9-volt battery
- small, flat screwdriver
- needle-nose pliers
- safety goggles
- notebook and pen

2. Put on your safety goggles. Hold the battery flat on a surface that won't be damaged by an errant screwdriver blade. Use the blade to bend out the metal flaps of the 9-volt battery. These flaps hold the bottom piece of cardboard in place. You will need to work all the way around the base, bending the metal outward, away from the bottom. Eventually, you will be able to pry out the cardboard. With a bit more pushing—watch your fingers so that you don't cut them with the screwdriver—you can extract the six batteries inside (Figure 2.3). Notice that they are connected in series.

Some interior batteries are arranged like a stack of rectangular pancakes, one on top of the others. Even though the arrangement is different, the batteries are connected in series, and each cell outputs 1.5 volts.

Disposing of Batteries

Tossing dead batteries into the trash will send them to a landfill where they not only take up space but also pose an environmental hazard. Over time the chemicals inside will leak out. Discarded batteries in landfills contribute about 88 percent of the mercury and 50 percent of the cadmium found in landfills. Both of these chemicals pose serious health and environmental risks. These nasty chemicals are useful to make electricity in a battery, but we don't want them getting into the ground. Do your part by not letting batteries get into the trash can. Find out from your local government or trash collection company how to dispose of them safely.

FIGURE 2.3 Inside a 9-volt battery you will find six small batteries connected in series.

Don't open the individual batteries as they do contain corrosive chemicals. Make sure you dispose of the battery parts as you would dispose of any other battery.

Direct Current

Batteries deliver electricity as a steady flow in one direction. Electrons flow from one battery terminal through the motor and back to the other battery terminal in a continuous flow. This is called direct current (DC).

The electricity that comes from your wall outlet isn't continuous: it alternates between flowing in one direction and then the other direction. This is called alternating current, or AC. In the United States, AC current completes 60 cycles per second.

Why Do We Use Alternating Current?

Early electric power companies, pioneered by Thomas Edison, supplied only direct current. As the power grids got larger, it became obvious that alternating current was more efficient. Alternating current can travel long distances with little energy loss in the wires, but direct current cannot. Edison's business model required building power plants every few miles throughout a city. That required shipments of coal throughout residential and business neighborhoods to the air-polluting plants. Switching to alternating current allowed very large plants to be built far away from the city, where space was available and less expensive. People didn't need to live next to noisy and dirty industrial plants.

Measure the Voltage of a Battery

1. Turn the voltmeter dial to measure DC volts. If there are several voltage ranges shown on the dial, use the one that is higher than the voltage you expect to be measuring.

2. Touch one of the voltmeter probes to one terminal of the battery and the other probe to the other terminal of the battery (see Figure 2.4). What voltage does the battery measure? Record this value in your notebook. Does the meter show a negative sign in front of the value? If you see a negative sign, switch the probes. That is, take the probe that is on the negative battery terminal and put it on the positive terminal, and place the other probe on the negative terminal. If your first measurement was negative, it should now be positive. Or, if your first measurement was positive, it should now be negative. Note that one of the probes is red and the other is black.

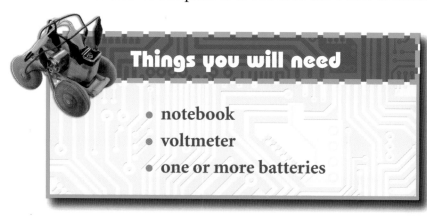

Things you will need

- notebook
- voltmeter
- one or more batteries

FIGURE 2.4 Use a voltmeter to measure the voltage of a battery.

The red probe connects to the positive side of the meter, and it is usually connected to the positive terminal of a battery. The black probe usually connects to the negative terminal of the battery. The meter will work if the probes are reversed, but you will see a negative sign in front of the voltage measurement.

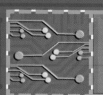

3. Measure other batteries and record what you find.

4. Look on the battery to find what the manufactured voltage is. Is this the same voltage you measured? If the battery is fresh, you might find the voltmeter registered a voltage higher than the value printed on the battery. If the battery has been used, you might find a value lower than the printed value. Batteries that have been used deliver lower voltages.

Voltage is a measure of electrical force. It tells us how hard a battery can push electrical energy through a motor. The higher the voltage, the harder a battery can push. A 9-volt battery has six times the pushing power of an AA or C battery.

Voltage measures how forceful the electricity is. The amount of electricity that flows, or current, is measured in amperes. The large the voltage, the greater the flow of current. However, a large voltage doesn't mean that the current is large. If you are pushing a shopping cart, the harder you push, the faster it goes. But if you are pushing it across a field of grass rather than the smooth floor of a store, your hard pushing won't move the cart as fast. The surface of the field provides a lot of resistance. The higher the resistance, the slower you will go.

Measure the Resistance of Common Materials

1. You can use a voltmeter to measure the resistance of a few materials. Turn the dial on the face of the voltmeter to the area that measures ohms (Ω). Be sure to record in your notebook the resistance that the meter shows along with the name of the material you are testing.

2. First touch the ends of the two voltmeter probes together. You should see the resistance is zero.

3. Now try measuring the resistance of a pencil. Keep the ends of the two probes away from each other on the pencil and record the value you read on the voltmeter. Then bring the two probes closer together and take another measurement.

4. Measure the resistance of a piece of wire. Record this value.

Things you will need

- notebook
- pencil
- voltmeter
- wire
- glass of water
- salt

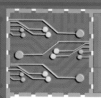

5. Fill a glass with water and measure the resistance with the two probes on opposite sides of the glass. Record the resistance.

6. Add some salt to the water and stir it so that it is completely dissolved. Measure the resistance again. Is the resistance different? Add more salt to see if the resistance changes.

Voltage, current, and resistance are all related. If the resistance remains unchanged, as the voltage increases, the current will increase. However, if the resistance increases, the current will decrease unless the voltage changes. Similarly, your shopping cart will slow down when you go from the store to the field unless you push a lot harder.

How Motors Work

There are many types of electric motors (see Figure 3.1). Many toys have inexpensive DC motors. Typically they are cylindrical. This book deals only with direct current (DC) motors—motors that can be powered by batteries.

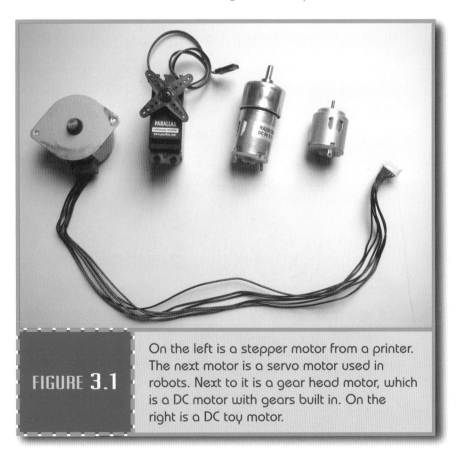

FIGURE 3.1 On the left is a stepper motor from a printer. The next motor is a servo motor used in robots. Next to it is a gear head motor, which is a DC motor with gears built in. On the right is a DC toy motor.

Examine a DC Motor

1. Pick up a DC motor. What do you notice? Is it light or heavy for its size? The weight suggests what you might find inside (and you will find out in the next experiment). Take notes on your observations and record them in your notebook.

2. Look at the metal outside. Do you see openings in this housing? Holes let air inside to keep the motor cool. Because the motor wastes a lot of energy in the form of heat, it needs to get rid of this heat through these openings.

3. Hold a paper clip near the motor. What do you notice? Is the paper clip attracted to the motor? What does that suggest is inside the motor?

Things you will need

- DC motor
- notebook and pen
- paper clip

4. Turn the motor shaft. Does it turn in steps or does it turn smoothly? Different types of DC motors operate differently. Some motors, called stepper motors, turn in tiny steps. Stepper motors are also used in robotics and are found commonly in printers. Rather than spin as a normal motor does, a stepper does as its name implies: it takes one step at a time. Each step is a fraction of a complete revolution. Twisting the motor shaft, you can feel it click at each step. The precise turn-and-stop nature of a stepper makes it ideal for pushing a piece of paper exactly one line forward. Steppers are easy to identify by their compact cylindrical shape and by the large number of electrical leads: 4 or more.

5. If the shaft turns smoothly, it is a typical DC motor. If it is difficult to turn, it might be a gearhead motor. These motors look like an elongated DC motor. They have a motor shaft at one end and two electrical contacts at the other. Inside, there is a DC motor and a set of gears. Twisting the motor shaft is difficult and may damage the gears. The gears reduce the speed of rotation by a factor of 50 to 100. So instead of spinning at 10,000 RPM (revolutions per minute), for example, a gearhead motor might spin at only 100 RPMs. Although a faster spinning motor might sound more attractive, many applications require the slower motion of a gearhead. Connected to a

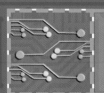

battery, the motor shaft turns slowly and you tend not to hear the high-pitch whine of the typical DC motor.

6. At the other end of the motor from the shaft, notice the two electrical contacts. These metal tabs are used to connect the motor to a battery. Do you find any markings that indicate which contact is supposed to connect to the positive or negative terminal of a battery? Servo motors have three electrical contacts. Servo motors are found in radio-controlled planes, boats, and sometimes cars. They are used extensively in robots. The benefit of a servo motor is that you can easily control its direction and speed by changing a control signal to it. If you tried to twist the motor shaft of a servo motor, you would find it difficult to do, and you could potentially damage the motor. Inside a servo motor is a small motor, a circuit board for interpreting the control signal, and a set of gears.

The motors used in most of the experiments in this book usually run on a voltage of 1.5 to 9 volts, and they spin at high speeds of 3,500 to 17,000 RPM. They spin quite a bit slower when a load is placed on them (when you make them do work). The higher the voltage you apply, the larger the current supplied to the motor and the faster it will spin, up to its maximum capacity. If you connect one to a battery, you will hear it hum at high speeds. You will also notice that it warms up.

The friction inside is considerable, and these motors are probably only 70 to 80 percent efficient. This means that 20 to 30 percent of the energy supplied from a battery is converted into heat through internal friction of parts rubbing on other parts. We'll peek inside this type of motor in Experiment 3.2.

Direct Current Brush Motors

How do you convert electrical energy from a battery into motion that can be used? A battery in a complete circuit sends out a steady stream of electrons in one direction. The chemical energy inside the battery provides the push to move the electrons down the wire. But how do you convert that stream of electrons into a spin?

The secret, discovered by physicist Michael Faraday, is that a coil of wire that has a current passing through it creates a magnetic force. Electromagnets are coils of wire wrapped around a piece of metal (iron or steel). Connected to a battery, this coil acts as a magnet. By changing the leads to the battery, the flow of electrons reverses, and so does the magnetic field.

The trick to making a DC motor is changing the magnetic force in electromagnets inside as the motor shaft spins. Placing a powerful permanent magnet inside the motor provides a strong force for the electromagnet to attract or repulse. As the motor shaft spins, the

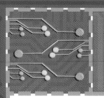

electromagnet attached to the shaft is attracted to one side of the permanent magnet and is repulsed by the other. If nothing changed, the spinning would stop when the opposite poles of the electromagnet and permanent magnet were closest. To keep the motor spinning, the magnetic force of the electromagnet changes, so it is always being repulsed by one end of the permanent magnet and attracted by the other.

The way to make this happen is to have a switch that changes the connection to the battery as the motor spins. This switch is called the commutator. It has conducting contacts mounted on the axle of the motor. These brush against contacts on the inside of the motor called brushes. Brushes connect to the terminals outside the motor. They are spring mounted, so they press against or brush the commutator to make contact. As the motor spins, the brushes carrying the electrical current touch different sets of contacts on the shaft. They allow the electromagnets to change polarity (positive to negative and back) just in time to attract and repel the permanent magnets.

Sound confusing? Let's take a motor apart to see all these pieces.

Take a Motor Apart

1. Look at the end of the motor—not the end where the motor shaft comes out, but the other end. Locate the two tiny metal tabs that hold the motor together. Connect these to a 9-volt battery. Does the motor work? (Its okay if it doesn't.)

2. Put on the gloves and safety goggles. Hold the motor in one hand and the screwdriver in the other. Force the tip of a flat-head screwdriver under the tabs and lever them up. This is the dangerous part: If you push on the end of the screwdriver, it can slip quickly past the motor into the hand that is holding it. Hold the motor on a table to keep it from moving while you pry up the tabs. Aim the screwdriver away from your hand so that if it slips, it doesn't hurt you.

Things you will need

- notebook
- toy motor
- small flat-head screwdriver
- safety goggles
- heavy gloves
- 9-volt battery

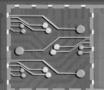

3. Once the tabs are raised, you can pull the white base from the metal covering. Find the electrical contacts that run through the white base. They are connected to two strips of metal that press against the motor shaft. Look at the ends of the strips. Do you see a lump of black material on each? These are the brushes (see Figure 3.2). They deliver electricity to the spinning motor. Look where they contact the shaft. Can you see the electrical contacts they touch?

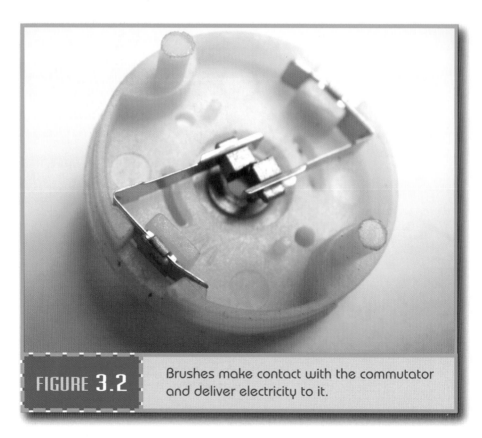

FIGURE 3.2 Brushes make contact with the commutator and deliver electricity to it.

4. Pull the motor shaft out of the case (see Figure 3.3). You will feel the resistance to your pulling. The magnets inside the motor case are resisting your removal of the motor shaft. Once the shaft is removed, look inside for the two magnets. You can extract these, but it may not be easy to do if they have been glued in place.

5. Look at the motor shaft. There are three coils of wires. These are the electromagnets. They get electrical energy from a battery through the motor contacts. The electricity flows through the brushes at the end of the contacts and to the spinning shaft. Look closely at the shaft where

FIGURE 3.3

Here are the parts of a DC motor. The two permanent magnets are housed on the inside of the metal case.

the brushes contact it. It is divided into sections. Each section supplies electricity to one of the three electromagnets. This part of the motor is called the commutator (see Figure 3.4). It acts as a switch to send the electricity to each of the three electromagnets at different times. As the shaft spins, each of the electromagnets is connected to the battery for only part of one revolution of the shaft. The electromagnets spin around, pulled toward and away from the permanent magnets inside the metal housing. By changing the electrical connections to the three electromagnets, the commutator keeps the motor spinning.

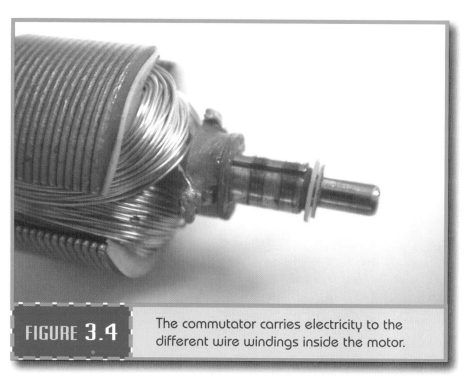

FIGURE **3.4**

The commutator carries electricity to the different wire windings inside the motor.

6. If the motor was working before you took it apart, try putting it back together. It's tricky to get the brushes back in place, but if you can do that, you can push the motor together and push the tabs down. Connect the motor to a 9-volt battery to see if it works.

Idea for a Science Fair Project

Many devices at home use motors. When one breaks and is going to be discarded, ask if you can have the motor inside. Remove the motor and any gearing or belts and pulleys that connects to it. Look at the motor for any written description. Many motors have descriptions that tell you what their operating voltages are. If the motor runs on low-voltage DC electricity (9 volts or less), try operating the motor with a 9-volt battery. If you were able to extract the entire assembly that the motor drives (gears, for example), see how they operate as you apply electricity to the motor. Then ask yourself how you could use the motor. What experiments could you run with the motor?

Make a Motor

Now that you have seen the inside of a motor and understand how it works, you can make one! There are many ways to make one with inexpensive materials. Here is one of the easiest (see Figure 3.5).

Things you will need

- 2 AA, C, or D batteries, or one 9-volt battery
- battery holders (optional, but they make it easier to connect the batteries)
- 2 wires or clip leads
- 3-inch block of wood and drill and drill bits, or a 6- or 8-ounce paper cup and masking tape
- several strong ceramic magnets (from an electronics stores)
- 2 feet of single-strand, 20-gauge magnet wire (from an electronics store)
- 2 large paper clips
- sandpaper
- marking pen
- cardboard
- wires or clip leads
- drill
- tape

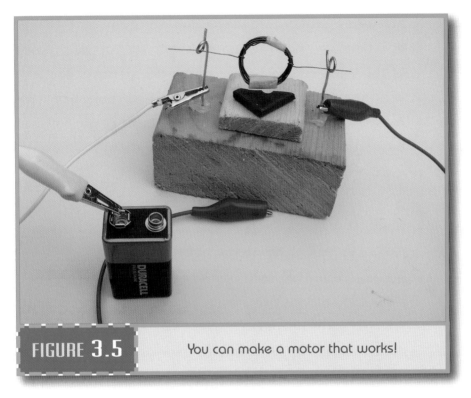

FIGURE 3.5   You can make a motor that works!

1. Start by rolling 2 feet of single-strand 20-gauge magnet wire loosely around your index finger, making neat coils. Finish by having the two opposite ends of the wire on opposite sides of the coil. Wrap each loose end around the coils three times to help hold them in place, but be sure to leave at least 2 inches of wire at each end of the coil.

2. Sand the insulation off each end of the loose wire. These exposed ends will become the electrical contacts. Along with the paper clips, they will become the commutator,

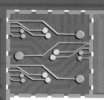

or sliding switch. Hold the coil vertically at the edge of a table so that you can reinsulate the top half of one of the loose ends. Use a marking pen to cover the wire with a layer of insulation (from the marking pen ink). Make sure you cover only the top half, while the coil is in the vertical position.

3. Assemble a support to hold the coil. Open two large paper clips so that one looped end of each can make a stand to support the coil. The straightened end of each paper clip will be inserted into the base.

4. If you're using a 3-inch block of wood for the base, drill small holes about two inches apart to set the clips in. If you are using a paper cup instead of a block of wood for the base, tape the straightened ends of the paper clips to the sides of the cup. Position the loop of each paper clip so that it is about 1¼ inches above the base.

5. Balance the coil so that it is supported at each end by one of the loops of a paper clip. Gently, push the coil so that it spins in a circle. Does it continue to spin or does it stop immediately? You want to adjust it so that it is balanced and rotates easily inside the loops. Bend the wire coil to make these adjustments.

6. Put one or more magnets on the top of the base, directly beneath the coil. Use folded paper or cardboard under the magnets to raise them so that they are close to the coil.

You want the magnets as close to the coil as you can get them without having them touch.

7. Now it's time to make the connections and test your motor. If you are using cylindrical batteries, place one in a battery holder. Use the wires or clip leads to connect each terminal of a battery or battery holder to one of the paper clips that is supporting the coil.

8. The coil may have started to spin on its own. If not, give it a slight flick to get it started. It should spin around.

9. The motor may not work the first time. If it does spin, pat yourself on the back. You have just built an electric motor. If it doesn't spin, check the battery connection and make sure the batteries have charge. (Test them in a flashlight or other battery-powered appliance.) Switch out the wire connectors—a surprisingly high number of bad connectors are sold. Make sure the magnets are very close to the coil and that the coil can spin freely. Recheck to see that you sanded all the insulation off the wire ends and that only the top half of one end has an insulating marker coating on it.

10. If the motor still doesn't work, try adding a second battery. Connect the battery cases in series. That is, connect the two batteries so that the positive end of one is wired to the negative end of the other. Then connect one of the loose contacts to one paper clip and the other contact to

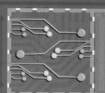

the second paper clip. Connecting the batteries in series increases the voltage in the circuit. For two C batteries, the circuit voltage will be 3 volts.

These motors spin slowly enough that you could count the number of revolutions it makes in 10 seconds. With the help of a friend, count and record the number of revolutions. Then change the voltage by increasing or decreasing the number of batteries you use to power the motor. See if you can still count the number of revolutions. Repeat this experiment again with a different voltage and graph your results (voltage and speed of rotation) to show how voltage affects the speed of rotation.

There are many other ways to make a simple motor. Can you think of a few variations of this model? Do a web search for simple motor designs to see what others have come up with.

Ideas for a Science Fair Project

Try some experiments with the motor. You can change the circuit voltage by increasing or decreasing the number of batteries. You can change the number and position of batteries. Or, you can make a new rotor that has twice as many coils. Does this one spin faster or slower than the first motor?

How Does Your Motor Work?

Just as in the motor you took apart, the motor you made has a permanent magnet and electromagnetic coils. Both have commutators. When you connect your motor to the battery, electrical current flows through the coils, creating a magnetic field. One end of the coils will have a positive polarity and the other negative. Free to spin, the coil will try to line up with the magnetic field created by the permanent magnet. Opposite poles attract and the same poles repel. If you had not marked one end of the wire, the coil would have positioned itself with one end close to the magnet and then stopped. By insulating half of the wire end, you created a rotating switch. As the coil spins, the current is blocked and the electromagnet loses its attraction for the permanent magnet. However, because it is spinning, it doesn't come to rest immediately. It spins until the wire end rotates past the insulated part and again conducts electricity. Then the electromagnet reenergizes and pulls the coil. Without sufficient momentum, the coil will not make complete circles, and it will soon stop.

How To Get Work From Motors

M ost motors provide mechanical motion in a circular direction: They spin. How do you transform that spinning into something useful?

Transferring motion is often the most difficult challenge in making things with electric motors. This chapter presents a variety of ways to transfer energy from the motor shaft to another moving part.

Direct Drive

Direct drive means that whatever you want to move is attached directly to the motor shaft. This sounds like the simplest solution, but often it isn't. Most of the inexpensive motors that you can use in projects spin at very high speeds and have very low torque, or turning power. Often you need just the opposite: lower speed and higher torque.

The other issue with direct drive is how to connect the thing you want to move to the motor shaft. A typical inexpensive motor has a shaft diameter of 2 mm. If you want to use direct drive, try to find something that has a mounting hole this size.

For example, you can make a propeller car or boat by mounting a propeller directly onto the motor shaft (see Chapters 6 and 7). Before purchasing a propeller, make sure

Things you will need

- motor
- wheel
- cocktail straw
- glue
- tape
- drill
- dowel

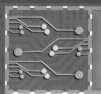

FIGURE 4.1 Attach a drive wheel directly to motor shaft so that it spins as the motor spins.

it accepts an axle diameter that matches your motor shaft diameter. At high speeds, a loose propeller will fly off the motor shaft, possibly injuring someone.

1. Try mounting a wheel directly onto the shaft of a motor (see Figure 4.1). If the motor shaft is smaller than the wheel opening, you can make a bushing or a coupler to connect two different-sized devices. If you had a wheel made for a ¼-inch axle, you could glue a ¼-inch dowel in the wheel and drill a 2-mm hole in the axle (dowel) to fit onto the motor shaft. This isn't easy (finding the exact center and drilling the hole exactly parallel to the dowel

length), so you might want to get some help to make bushings.

2. If the motor shaft isn't long enough, you can extend it with a cocktail straw (see Figure 4.2). These fit loosely on a 2-mm motor shaft. To make a tighter fit, wrap the motor shaft with a small piece of masking tape and then force the straw over the tape. If the straw still slides, add a drop of glue to the top of the masking tape and then quickly force the straw onto the shaft.

FIGURE 4.2 This boat propeller uses a cocktail straw to extend the motor shaft so that the propeller can reach the water while keeping the motor dry.

Make a Belt Drive

Using a rubber band to connect the motor and wheels or axles has some big advantages. Rubber bands allow you to connect different-sized axles as long as the motor shaft is nearly parallel to the driveshaft. If the driveshaft has a much larger diameter than the motor shaft, the rubber band also provides gearing, or slowing down, of the motion. By crossing the rubber band into a figure eight, you reverse the direction in which the drive axle spins.

The difficulty with using belt drives is getting the right tension on the belt. If the belt is too loose, the motor will spin and the belt won't turn. If the belt is too tight, it can

Things you will need

- a partner
- cardboard box
- scissors or screwdriver to make holes in the cardboard
- small electric motor
- ¼-inch dowel
- wide rubber band
- 2 or 4 batteries
- battery holders
- cardboard tube
- glue or tape
- clip leads

stop the motor from spinning. Before fixing the motor in place, test various positions to see where your rubber band belt will best spin the axle.

The other challenge is keeping the rubber band belt on the driveshaft. As the motor spins, the rubber band tends to slide along the shaft, and it can slide all the way off. To prevent this, position the motor so that when the belt slides, it slides toward the motor and not toward the end of the shaft. You could also use a pulley on the motor shaft (see Figure 4.3) to help anchor the belt.

FIGURE 4.3 A pulley can slide onto the shaft of a motor to help hold a belt (rubber band) in place.

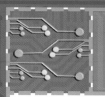

1. Make one hole in each of two opposite sides of a small cardboard box. Slide a ¼-inch dowel through the first hole and loop a rubber band around it. The rubber band will be the drive belt that takes rotational energy from the motor and turns the device you are building.

2. Push the dowel through the second hole so that it is held in place by the two holes. The dowel is now an axle. Loop the rubber band around the motor shaft. With some help, connect the battery to the motor. Play with the tension in the rubber band to find the best distance between the motor and the dowel.

3. Glue or tape the motor to the bottom of the box at this distance.

4. Try using a larger axle. Slide a cardboard tube (from a roll of paper towels or a mailing tube) onto the axle and loop the rubber band around it. Does it spin faster or slower than the wood dowel did? If you have trouble seeing how fast the tube spins, mark it with a pen.

5. Try increasing the voltage supplied by the battery. Use a battery holder to hold 2 or 4 AA, C batteries, or D batteries and connect the holder to the motor. How does the motor react to different voltages?

Make a Pulley Set

COOL!

Pulleys (see Figure 4.4) help hold a belt on to a motor shaft or driveshaft and can provide some gearing. They will have a diameter larger than the shaft to which they are connected. You can purchase pulleys from science catalogs. Check to see that a pulley shaft hole is the same size as the axles or motor shafts you are using. If you can't find a match, is there a bushing that will fit both the pulley and the shaft? You can also find pulleys in old machinery that you take apart (check garage sales and thrift shops for broken appliances) and in hardware stores.

If you don't have a pulley, you can glue two wheels together side by side to form one. You may need to put a

Things you will need

- 4 toy wheels, 2 each of two different sizes
- cardboard
- scissors
- rubber bands
- dowels or pencils
- color marking pen
- glue
- cardboard box

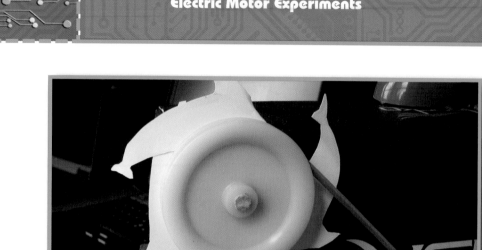

FIGURE **4.4**   Pulleys allow you to transfer spinning energy from one axle to another.

cardboard spacer between the two wheels to provide a valley in which the rubber band (belt) can ride.

1. Cut a piece of cardboard into a circle that is about ¼ inch smaller in diameter than one of the pairs of wheels. Poke a hole through the center of it.

2. Glue it between the two wheels. When the glue is dry, test the pulley to see if the cardboard is centered and the glue is holding.

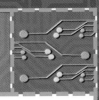

3. Make a second pulley from the other two wheels. To test them in a cardboard box, poke holes through the sides of the box to support one axle (dowel or pencil) with the first pulley attached to it. Before placing the axle in position, loop a large rubber band on the pulley.

4. Stretch the rubber band to get an idea of where a second axle and pulley should be located. The two axles need to be far enough apart so that the rubber band is taut, but not so far apart that it causes the axles to bend. Once you have decided its position, install the second axle, first looping the rubber band around the pulley.

5. Test your pulley system. Turn one pulley to see if the rubber band turns the other pulley.

6. Spin the larger pulley one revolution and count how many times the smaller pulley turns. Then spin the smaller pulley one time to see how far the larger one turns. The larger the difference in size, the greater their gear ratio. To help see when each pulley has completed a turn, mark a line on them using a colored marking pen.

   Having a large pulley on the motor shaft and a small pulley on the axle of whatever you are turning will spin the drive axle faster than the motor. Reversing this gearing so that the smaller pulley is on the motor shaft will cause the drive axle to spin slower (see Figure 4.5).

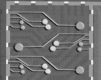

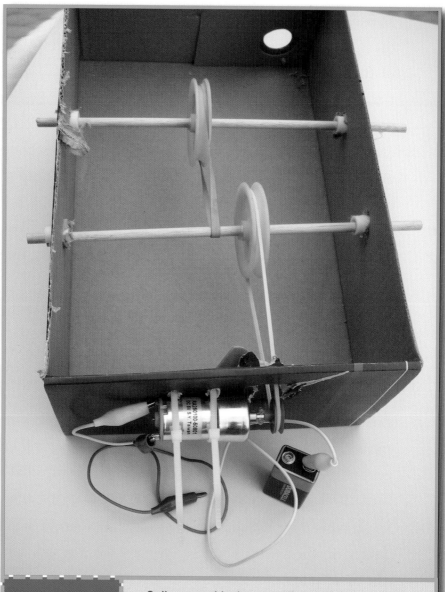

FIGURE 4.5 Pulleys and belts can allow you to reduce or increase the speed of the motor's rotation.

Make a Cam

Motors spin, but sometimes the motion you want is up and down or back and forth. Cams provide one way of getting linear motion from circular motion. If you have a wheel centered on an axle, like the front wheel on a bike, it spins in circles. But if the axle supports the wheel anyplace except for the exact center of the wheel, the wheel spins in an odd

Things you will need

- **an adult**
- **wood wheels, circles cut from cardboard, or plastic lids from food containers**
- **drill bit**
- **drill**
- **axles (dowels or pencils)**
- **cardboard box (from Experiment 4.2)**
- **cardboard**

- scissors
- ruler
- glue
- electric motor (gearhead motor if possible)
- rubber band
- electric belt drive (from Experiment 4.2)

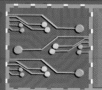
shape (see Figure 4.6). The farther from the center that the axle is positioned, the more exaggerated its motion would be. If you could magically balance a stick so that it always points upward and rides on the top of the wheel, it would move up and down. You would have transformed the circular motion of a wheel into vertical motion.

FIGURE **4.6**

A cam can be made by drilling an off-center hole in a circle or wheel. An axle is inserted through this new hole. When a cam rotates, it lifts whatever is above it.

1. **Ask an adult** to either drill a ¼-inch hole or poke a hole near the outer edge of a wooden wheel or cardboard or plastic circle. This is your cam.

2. Use a cardboard box from Experiment 4.2. In this case, slide one end of a dowel or pencil (that becomes the axle) through the first hole in the box. Slide the cam onto the axle and then push the axle through the other side of the box. If the cam doesn't fit tightly on the axle, glue it in place.

3. Twist the axle by hand to see the cam action. As the axle rotates the cam will rotate, but its rotation will not be symmetrical around the axle. If you were standing on a platform that touched the edge of the cam, you would be raised and lowered as the cam rotates.

4. To make this into a usable cam, cut a 3-inch-diameter circle out of cardboard and glue it onto the end of a dowel. This device is a cam follower. The follower will ride up and down as the cam turns.

5. Poke a hole in the top of the box, directly above the cam. Insert the cam follower through the hole so that it rests on the cam. As you turn the axle, the follower and its shaft will ride up and down. You may need to make a "bearing" to keep the follower on track.

6. Drill a hole in a piece of heavy cardboard and glue this on top of the box, so that the hole aligns with the hole

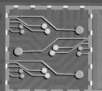

for the cam follower. Then put the cam follower back into the hole. The additional cardboard will help guide the cam follower up and down.

7. Now try using the electric belt drive from the previous experiment to turn the cam. A slower motor, a gearhead motor (see Figure 4.7), will work better here.

FIGURE **4.7** A gearhead motor is a DC motor with internal gears that delivers a slower rate of rotation.

Make a Crank

COOL!

Another way to get linear motion from a motor is with cranks. As you rotate a crank, it provides back-and-forth or up-and-down motion (see Figure 4.8). Cranks can also make it easier to turn an axle. Turning an axle by hand is hard. A hand crank improves your turning power by giving you a lever to rotate around the axle (see Figure 4.9).

1. Use the same box used in the previous two experiments. Ask **an adult** to use a coping saw to cut three pieces off of a dowel. Two of the pieces should be longer than half the width of the box, and the third piece should be 2 inches long.

Things you will need

- **an adult**
- **cardboard box (from Experiment 4.2)**
- **dowel or pencils**
- **coping saw**
- **cardboard, thin wood, or plastic**
- scissors
- glue
- drill and drill bit
- safety goggles
- stiff wire

FIGURE **4.8**

A crank, like a cam, can change circular motor into up and down motion.

FIGURE **4.9**

A hand crank makes it easier to turn an axle. It provides additional turning power or torque.

2. Use two pieces of stiff material, such as cardboard, thin wood, or plastic. Cut the pieces about 4 inches long and ¾ inch wide.

3. **Ask an adult** to drill or poke ¼-inch holes in both ends of the two pieces of stiff material. Force one of the long dowels into one hole of one of the pieces of stiff material. Force the other long dowel into one of the holes in the other piece of stiff material. Glue the dowels in these holes. Then force the short piece of dowel into the two remaining holes so that the two pieces of stiff material are parallel to each other. Glue this dowel in both pieces. You'll have to do this after the dowels are inside the box with the free ends passing through the holes.

4. As you hand-twist the dowel, the crank rises and falls. To get useful motion out of this, wrap a piece of stiff wire around the short dowel and have it protrude through the hole in the top of the box (from the preceding experiment). As you turn the axle, the wire rises and falls.

5. Add a second crank to the end of one of the long pieces of dowel. Cut another piece of stiff material and drill holes in each end. Force the material onto the end of the long dowel. Insert another short section of dowel into the other hole. The short dowel allows you to easily rotate the axle.

Make a Gear Set

Gears connect motors to many different tools. They can slow down or speed up the motion of the tools. They can change the direction of the motion and, with a rack, they can convert circular motion into linear motion.

You can make your own gears (see Figure 4.10), but for more precise motion you might want to purchase gear sets from a science supply store or catalog. Part of the difficulty of using gears with motors is holding the gears in position so that they mesh with the motor and with adjacent gears. You can overcome this by getting a complete system that includes mounting brackets.

Things you will need

- an adult
- cardboard
- scissors
- craft sticks
- coping saw
- drill and drill bit, or nail punch
- ¼-inch dowel
- glue

| FIGURE 4.10 | You can make your own gears from cardboard and craft sticks. |

1. Cut two large (2-inch-diameter) and two small (1-inch-diameter) circles out of cardboard. Ask **an adult** to poke or drill a center hole (1/4 inch) in each.

2. With **an adult**'s help, use a coping saw to cut large craft sticks in half.

3. Glue the edges of 8 craft stick pieces on the larger circle and 4 or 6 on the smaller circle, whichever gives about the same spacing of pieces as on the larger circle. Apply the glue to the edges of the craft sticks and place them so

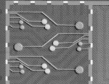

that they stand on edge and radiate from the center of each circle.

4. Slide a piece of ¼-inch dowel through the two large circles. Repeat this process with the smaller pair of circles. Glue the matching size circle to the opposite edges of the craft sticks. Hold tightly while the glue dries (or use rubber bands to hold them together). Having the dowel in place aligns the two wheels while you are gluing them.

5. Use a small cardboard box to mount these gears. Mount one gear on its dowel/axle so that the axle is supported by holes in opposite ends of the box. When it is in place, mount the second axle parallel to the first one, so that the two sets of teeth (craft sticks) will fit together, allowing both gears to turn.

6. Turning one gear should turn the other gear in the opposite direction. Try turning the larger gear while counting the number of rotations the smaller gear makes. The gear ratio is the number of teeth on the first gear divided by the number on the second gear. If your first gear has 8 teeth and the second, smaller gear has 4 teeth, the ratio is 2:1. The smaller gear should rotate twice as fast as the larger one.

7. Try running the gears the other way. Turn the smaller gear and count the number of times the larger gear rotates.

With gears, cranks, pulleys, and cams, you can harness the power of motors and put it to use. Think of some useful or artistic and fun ways to use these components. With just a few ideas, start building and change your design as you go. You will be prototyping with electric motors!

Ideas for a Science Fair Project

Find other common materials you can use to make teeth and gears. Craft sticks work adequately but have a lot of friction as the teeth of opposing gears rub together. Can you find plastics to replace the craft sticks? How could you test the effectiveness of gears and demonstrate which material or gear design works best?

Circuits

You can make a direct connection between a motor and battery by connecting the contacts or terminals of each. In many machines, however, if you physically separate the two, you will achieve a better balance to whatever you are building. Sometimes there isn't space for both battery and motor at the same place. To connect motor and battery electrically while keeping them apart from each other, conductors or wire connectors are used.

Wires provide very low resistance connections between electric components. For many applications, alligator clip leads are the best wires to use. They connect instantly to battery cases and to the terminals of transistor batteries, and they connect to motor terminals. You can do projects without them, but having a few pairs of them will make it faster to connect the electrical circuits.

Don't leave wires or clip leads connected to a battery case or battery when you aren't using the power. If the two leads come in contact with each other or both contact another conductor, they will drain or possibly short circuit the battery.

Connect the Motor

1. Connect one terminal of a small motor to a battery terminal (or terminal of a battery holder) and the other motor terminal to the other battery terminal (see Figure 5.1). You should hear a whirring as the motor spins. Look to see which way the motor spins. If you're not sure, gently touch the spinning shaft.

If the motor isn't spinning, check the connections. Wire connectors can break (alligator clip leads much more than wire), so try a different clip lead for one connection and then the second. Is the battery fresh? Sometimes you will find a dead battery even in a previously unopened box, so replace the battery. If neither of these is the problem, spin the motor shaft between your thumb and fingers. If it is sluggish or doesn't turn at

Things you will need

- small motor
- batteries
- battery holders
- clip leads

FIGURE 5.1 Use two clip leads or wires to connect the terminals of a battery to the motor terminals.

all, it is defective. Try a different motor. If the motor is one you extracted from a discarded appliance, check the voltage requirement (usually printed on the side). Make sure it uses DC current at a voltage that the battery can deliver. A motor that requires 24 volts won't turn with the 1.5 volts delivered by a C cell battery.

2. When you know which direction (clockwise or counterclockwise) the motor is spinning, disconnect the wires to the battery and reverse them. Take the wire that was connected to the positive side of the battery (see the + on the side of the battery) and clip it on the negative side. Take the wire from the negative side and clip it on the positive side. The motor should be spinning again. Check the direction of rotation. In what direction is it spinning?

3. Now connect the motor to other batteries. If you used a 9-volt battery first, now try a AA, C, or D cell. Having a few battery holders (see Figure 5.2) on hand would be helpful, but if you don't you can clip leads to paper clips and hold these to the ends or terminals of the battery (see Figure 5.3). For longer operation, use a rubber band to attach large paper clips to each terminal.

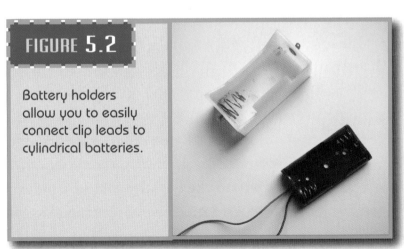

FIGURE 5.2

Battery holders allow you to easily connect clip leads to cylindrical batteries.

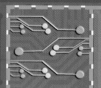

FIGURE 5.3

Instead of buying battery holders, you can make your own with large paper clips and a rubber band.

4. What do you notice? Does the motor spin faster or slower with different batteries? Try a few experiments to see if you can determine how the battery voltage and speed are related.

You can combine several batteries together to get different voltages. For example, you can connect two D cell batteries to give 3 volts of output. Connect the + end of one to the – end of the second one. Connect the + end of the second one to the motor and run the last wire from the other motor terminal to the – end of the first battery. This is a series connection where you connect the positive end of one battery to the negative end of another (see Figure 5.4). Don't get carried away increasing the voltage above the level that the motor is rated.

FIGURE 5.4

Connecting batteries in series increases the voltage in a circuit.

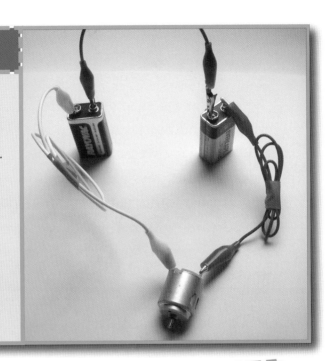

Idea for a Science Fair Project

Direct current motors will spin faster when the voltage applied is higher. You could conduct an experiment starting with one 1.5-volt battery powering a motor. Then add batteries to see how fast the motor will spin. You need a way to measure the motor's speed. One way is to use an electric-powered model car and measure how fast it moves across the floor a set distance. Record the time for three runs and then repeat with an additional battery of the same voltage. Graph the results, as speed (distance divided by time) vs. the voltage used.

Measure Voltages

1. If you have access to a voltmeter, try using it to measure voltages and resistances. Turn the meter dial to DC volts and put the two probes on the terminals of a 9-volt battery. What does the meter show?

2. If you have connected the positive probe to the negative terminal the meter will show a negative voltage. Switch the position of the two probes and try again. Does it read more than 9 volts? A fresh battery will have a voltage higher than its rating. If it has been used a lot, its voltage will be lower than its rating. Alkaline batteries tend to hold their voltage near their rating throughout the useful life of the battery, while older carbon batteries tend to gradually lose voltage with use.

Things you will need

- voltmeter
- motor
- 9-volt battery
- 2 clip leads

3. Now connect the battery to a motor (as in Experiment 5.1) and measure the voltage of the battery. Is it the same value you measured when the battery wasn't powering the motor? As soon as electricity is flowing from a battery to power a motor, the voltage measured drops. When you disconnect one of the wires to the motor, the battery voltage will rise to near its earlier value.

5.3

Add Resistance to the Circuit

1. Switch a voltmeter to measure resistance. On many meters the resistance setting is shown by a Greek letter omega (Ω). With the meter in this position, touch the two probes together. The reading should be zero.

2. Touch the two probes to your skin. Put them about one inch apart. You will get different readings depending on how moist or dry your skin is. Try moistening your skin with some saliva. The resistance should be much lower.

3. Test some other materials. Put the two probes on a piece of paper, cloth, wood, plastic, and metal (try a piece of

Things you will need

- notebook
- voltmeter
- motor
- battery
- clip leads
- paper clip
- aluminum foil
- paper, cloth, wood, and plastic substances
- craft stick
- glass of water
- salt

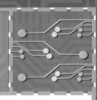

aluminum foil and a paper clip). Never put the probes on a battery when the meter is turned to measure resistance. This will damage the meter. From this experiment, which material conducts electricity well and which don't conduct electricity at all? Record your observations in your notebook.

4. Now see how resistance affects a motor. Using the motor/ battery circuit from Experiment 5.2, test the materials you used in Step 3. Use a clip lead to connect one end of a paper clip to one battery terminal and another clip lead to connect the other end of the paper clip to the motor. Use a third clip lead to connect the remaining terminal on the motor to the terminal on the battery. Does the motor spin? Does it appear to spin as rapidly as it did without having the paper clip in the circuit? Measure the voltage of the battery while it is powering the motor and record this value.

5. Test the other materials and record your observations.

6. Remove the material (wood, plastic, or metal) from the circuit and put the ends of the clip leads into a glass of water. Does the motor spin when the connections are made to the battery and motor? Measure the resistance of the water with the voltmeter. Record this value. What happens to the motor as you add salt to the glass of water? How much salt is needed before the motor

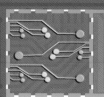

spins rapidly? Disconnect the battery and measure the resistance of the salt water and record this.

7. Use your data to calculate the current flowing through the various materials. Divide the voltage of the battery by the resistance of each material you tested to get the current in amperes that is flowing through the circuit. If the resistance was very high, the motor probably did not spin at all and the current you calculate will be zero or very, very small.

Make a Switch

Rather than clipping or attaching wires each time you want to operate a motor, you could make a switch (see Figure 5.5). You can purchase a variety of switches at electronics stores or from science supply houses. Here is one way to make your own.

1. Poke a hole through a piece of cardboard. Insert an acorn brass fastener through the end of a paper clip and into the cardboard hole. Spread the legs of the fastener so that it won't come out.

2. With a pencil, make a mark at the other end of the paper clip and poke a hole there.

3. Insert a second acorn fastener, spreading the legs of the fastener on the underside of the cardboard.

4. Attach wires or clip leads to each of the brass fasteners.

Things you will need

- clip leads or wires
- cardboard
- pencil
- acorn brass fasteners
- paper clip
- aluminum foil

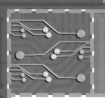

FIGURE 5.5

You can make switches out of common materials, such as paper clips and brass fasteners.

5. When you want the switch closed (to complete the circuit), swing the paper clip so that it contacts the second fastener. With the switch open, no current flows.

You can also use aluminum foil as a contact to make switches. Wrap bare wire around a craft stick and cover both with a piece of aluminum foil. Make a second contact (aluminum foil wrapped around a bare wire that is wrapped on a craft stick). Anchor the foil on each stick with a rubber band. Connect the two aluminum foil sections of the craft sticks to close the switch.

See how many other ways you can make switches with things in your house.

Making Cars Go

Now that you know how to make electric circuits, you are ready to use them in making models powered by electric motors.

A fun thing to do with an electric motor is to make a model car. You already know how to connect a motor to its power source, a battery. Now you can explore the various ways of using the mechanical energy from the motor to make a car go.

Make a Model Car

1. For a model car frame, use a piece of cardboard, egg carton top, old toy, or piece of wood. Cut the material into a rectangle about 4 inches wide and 6 inches long.

2. You will need three, four, or more wheels. It is best to purchase plastic or wood wheels and dowels that fit them (sources for these are listed in the appendix), or you may have some wheels and axles from toys. You could also make wheels following these steps: Use a compass or any manufactured cylinder to trace a circle on a piece of cardboard. The compass is better because it leaves a mark at the center where the axle will go. If the axle is off center, the wheel will wobble (act like a cam) and the car will move more slowly. Cut out the number of wheels you need for the car you want to build.

Things you will need

- cardboard, egg carton, old toy, or piece of wood
- scissors
- wheels or drawing compass
- dowels
- glue and tape
- straws or screw eyes

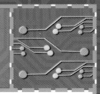

3. Most purchased wheels will fit either an ⅛-inch or ¼-inch dowel. The wheels will probably fit snugly onto the dowel. If not, use a small dab of hot glue on the axle. Then slide the wheel over the glue and into position on the axle.

4. You want the dowel to turn so that the car can move, so you cannot glue the axle to the car frame. You need the axle to be able to turn inside a tube or pipe. A standard drinking straw works well for ⅛-inch dowels. A milkshake or fat straw works for ¼-inch dowels. You might also check the plastic pipes and tubing at a hardware store. Plastic tubing is easy to cut and easy to glue in place. One last option is to support the axle with screw eyes—closed hooks that you can screw into a piece of wood.

5. For the car to be stable and travel in a straight line, you need to think about where to attach the bearings (straws/plastic tube) that hold the axles. If the two axles are close to each other in the center of the car, the ends of the car might tip up or down. If the axles are not parallel to each other, the car will turn consistently to one side. Tape the axles in place and experiment with the car. You can easily remove the tape and replace the axles. When they are in the place you want, glue the bearings to the bottom of the car frame. Now you're ready to add a motor.

Propeller Drive

The easiest drive system is one that doesn't depend on wheel traction. This model uses a propeller to blow air (see Figure 6.1). The car moves in the direction opposite to the direction the air is blown. Newton's second law states that for every action there is an equal and opposite reaction. In this case the action is pushing air in one direction. The propeller pushes air, so the air exerts an equal and opposite force on the propeller: the air pushes the propeller in the opposite direction.

1. Attach the propeller to the motor. See Experiment 4.1 for how to do this.

Things you will need

- notebook
- cardboard
- scissors
- motor
- propeller
- 9-volt battery
- clip leads
- car frame from Experiment 5.1
- meterstick
- stopwatch
- a partner

FIGURE **6.1**   The easiest electric car model to build is one powered by a propeller.

2. Use clip leads to connect a motor that has a propeller to a 9-volt battery. Feel both the flow of air and the direction the motor is being pushed. Disconnect the leads.

3. Set the motor with propeller on the car frame you made in Experiment 5.1. Check to see if the propeller will clear the ground. If it will hit the ground, make a motor mount out of cardboard to elevate the motor high enough to keep the propeller from hitting the ground.

4. Use a small bit of hot glue or some masking tape to hold the motor to the mount or car frame. Make sure the propeller is pointing directly backward. Figure out where

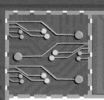

you should mount the battery to give the model balance between the weight of the motor and the battery. Use a small dab of glue or a piece of tape to hold the battery to the model frame.

5. Reconnect the clip leads. Be careful, as a fast-spinning propeller can hurt if it catches your finger. Release the model on the floor and watch what happens. Does it travel in a straight line? Is it fast?

6. What happens if the propeller isn't blowing directly to the rear of the car? Take an extreme example: What happens if the propeller is facing to the right? Remount the motor/propeller so that it pushes at right angles to the direction that car can go. Note what happens. If the car were on a frictionless surface—say a sheet of flat ice—what would happen if the propeller pushes to the one side?

7. Set up a test track on a smooth floor. Put a piece of masking tape on the floor for the start line. Three meters away, put a second piece of tape for the finish line. With the help of a friend, time how long it takes your car to go from the start to finish lines (see Figure 6.2). Repeat this experiment three times and average the times. That is, add the three times and divide by 3. Record the test results in your notebook.

FIGURE 6.2 Have a friend help you time how fast your car goes.

Idea for a Science Fair Project

Test a variety of propellers to see which pushes the car fastest. Check science and model sites and stores for propellers or make your own. Test either the number of blades, the size of the blades, or the total area of the blades. Graph your results showing the car's speed (distance of your experimental course divided by elapsed time) vs. the size or number of blades. Do you see a pattern?

Forces have direction. Pushing in one direction makes the car go in that direction. However, the friction between the wheels and the ground prevent the car from being pushed sideways. The wheels can move easily only when the car is pushed forward or backward. Pushing toward one side doesn't contribute to the car's motion.

What other experiments could you try? You could lay out a measured course and time your car to compute its speed. Repeating this several times would give you a speed measurement that averaged out some of the imperfections of any one measurement. Then you could try:

- changing the voltage by changing the type or number of batteries powering the car.

- using wheels of different sizes.

- switching the position of the wire contacts on the battery. Take the wire connected to the + side of the battery and now connect it to the – side. Complete the circuit with the other wire. What do you think will happen? See if the car is faster or slower.

- testing what happens if you add weight to your car (for example, a stack of quarters taped together). You can increase the number of quarters in the stack and see if the results change as the stack increases.

- testing if a spoiler or airfoil mounted over the wheels improves the speed.

- testing a parachute to see how much it slows the car.

- adding a second motor and propeller powered by the same battery.

Come up with other experiments to run. Make one modification to you car and time it on your test track. Record the times for at least three runs and average them. Compare them to your first run. Remember that if you do a lot of experiments, the battery will lose some power and the car will slow.

EHPERIMENT

6.3

COOL!

A Three-Wheel Car with Direct Drive

This model has a wheel mounted directly on the motor shaft (see Figure 6.3). Most likely the axle hole in the wheel will be much larger than the diameter of the motor shaft. You will need to secure the smaller shaft in the center of the wheel opening. If you use a 9-volt battery, the motor and attached wheel will spin so fast that the wheel will slide over the floor. You might need to add weight directly above the wheel to help it stay in contact with the ground.

1. For your first direct-drive car, use three wheels. You can try different models later, but in this case, a three-wheel car will be easier to make. The single wheel at one end

Things you will need

- **an adult**
- **notebook**
- **cardboard**
- **motor**
- **clip leads**
- **battery**
- **wheels**

- **axles (dowels)**
- **straws**
- **glue and tape**
- **drill**
- **rubber band**
- **washers or quarters**

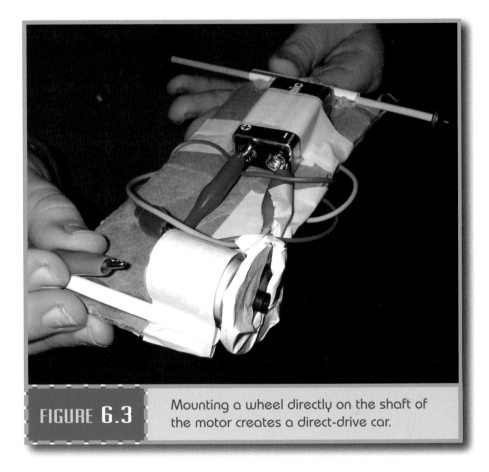

Mounting a wheel directly on the shaft of the motor creates a direct-drive car.

will be the drive wheel. Do you want front-wheel drive or rear-wheel drive? Does it make a difference in the speed?

2. Pick one wheel to become the drive wheel. Is there a way to connect the motor directly to a wheel? The motor shaft and wheel hole probably aren't the same size. If they are close, you can wrap some masking tape around

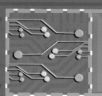

the motor shaft to get a tighter fit. If the wheel hole is much larger than the motor shaft, try inserting a tight-fitting dowel into the wheel hole and, with **an adult's** help, drilling a hole in the center of the dowel that fits the motor shaft.

3. To make a three-wheel car, cut a notch in the cardboard frame along the center of one end. The wheel can fit into the notch, and you can glue or tape the motor to the frame.

4. Does the frame need additional support to hold the weight of the motor?

5. Test the car and compare its speed to the speed of the propeller car (from Experiment 6.2). Run the experiment three times, and then average the times. Is the direct-drive model faster than the propeller model? Try the cars on different floor coverings. How does the direct-drive car do on very smooth floors compared to the propeller car? On carpets, how does each car do?

6. With the direct-drive car, if the drive wheel spins on a smooth surface, what can you do to improve its grip? Could you add a rubber band around the rim? Would adding some weight (try washers or quarters) directly above the wheel help? Give these a try to find out.

7. Can you make a model that has two of the wheels powered directly by motors? Can you get it to travel in a straight line?

Idea for a Science Fair Project

Test other wheels on your car. You could make wheels from one material and test the size of wheels vs. the speed of the car. Or you could try different materials of the same size.

Belt Drive

Can you think of a vehicle that uses a belt to transfer power to the drive wheels? In the early twentieth century, many trucks had chain drives. If you look under the hood of a car, you will find several belts that transfer power. Factories used to use belts to deliver power to machines before electricity was common. Bicycles and motorcycles have chain drives. Belt or chain drives are a very efficient way to transfer energy from a power source to wheels.

Things you will need

- notebook
- cardboard
- motor
- clip leads
- battery
- wheels, including an empty soda can
- axles (dowels)

- straws
- glue and tape
- rubber bands
- craft sticks (optional)
- stopwatch
- a partner
- pulley (optional)

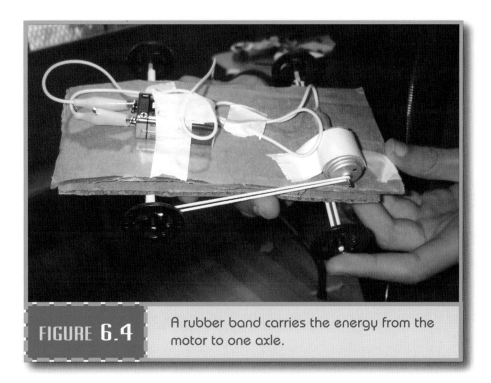

FIGURE **6.4**	A rubber band carries the energy from the motor to one axle.

1. Try making a model that uses belt drive (see Figure 6.4). Follow the same building process you used in earlier car models. For this model, connect the motor to the driveshaft with a rubber band.

2. Rubber bands make great belts. You can loop them over the motor shaft and axle and adjust the motor's position to get the right tension on the belt. An improvement is to use a pulley on the motor shaft to hold the belt in place. The belt fits in the pulley and tension keeps it from

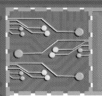

sliding out. You can find pulleys that fit the diameter of your motor shaft in science catalogs.

3. Other ways to keep the belt on the motor shaft are to use a thread spool or wheel. Empty soda cans make good wheels. Use wood wheels glued to the top and bottom of the can to hold the axle in place. Poke holes through the top and bottom of the can to let the axle come through. Add several additional rubber bands to the can to give it more traction.

4. If the belt (rubber band) slides off the motor shaft, realign the motor so that its shaft points slightly away from the axle it is driving. With this adjustment, the belt will slide toward the motor instead of away from it.

5. If the tension is too great, the motor may not spin or the wheels may not turn. In this case, move the motor closer or use a different-sized rubber band. High belt tension may cause the car frame to buckle. You may need to reinforce the frame with cardboard or craft sticks.

6. With a partner, time your car on the test track and calculate its average speed over three or more trials. How does it compare to the other models? Record your measurements in your notebook.

Gear Drive

Inexpensive toy motors spin much too quickly for controlled driving, and they don't provide much torque or turning power. Radio-controlled cars have gears to slow the speed of the rotation of the motor. By using a set of gears, the manufacturers reduce the speed and increase the torque.

To use gear drive, you could either add a set of gears to an inexpensive motor or use a gearhead motor. A gearhead motor has the gearing mounted in a case along with the motor. The advantage of the gearhead is that it is ready to

Things you will need

- notebook
- cardboard
- motor
- clip leads
- battery
- wheels
- axles (dowels)
- straws
- glue and tape
- gears or gearhead motor
- stopwatch
- partner
- table
- blocks

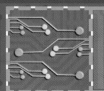

go out of the box. Just connect it to a battery and you have a reduced speed, higher torque output.

If you assemble your own set of gears, put them together so that the motor speed is reduced. Mount a small gear on the motor shaft and have it drive a larger gear on the axle, or if the wheel has gear teeth, have it drive the wheel itself (see Figure 6.5). Purchasing a set of gears and a frame to mount them on gives you more options. You can try different combinations of gears to get different speeds.

1. Using either a set of gears that you assemble or a gear-head motor, make a model using a gear drive. Make a new car body as described in Experiment 6.1, or reuse one of the car bodies you made earlier. The gears' driveshaft will rotate too slowly for a propeller drive (on a car), but could work well with either direct or belt drive.

2. If you are using a wheel that has gear teeth, you can add the wheel/axle assemblies. If you are using a gear on the drive axle, install it on the axle to get a better idea of where it will have to be located to mesh with the small gear on the motor.

3. Lay out the gears and motor to see where the motor needs to sit to reach either the gear on the drive axle or a geared wheel. Mark this location. Before gluing the motor, recheck the fit between motor and gear to be sure

FIGURE **6.5**   A small gear fits onto the motor shaft and meshes with the gears on a wheel.

that the gears will mesh when the car is sitting on the ground. Then glue the motor in place.

4. Connect the clip leads to the motor

5. Once you have the model built, ask a partner to help you test it on your test track. You might expect it to go much more slowly than earlier models. Measure how fast it travels over the test track you used for earlier models.

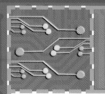
Repeat the experiment three times and average the times. Record the average time in your notebook.

6. Try it going uphill. Raise the legs on one end of a table and see if the gear drive car can climb your hill. Repeat the test for the cars that didn't have gear drive. Can the gear drive climb a steeper hill?

Shake Drive

Here is a vehicle just for fun. Unlike the previous versions, in this one the motor won't push air to move the car and it won't be connected to the wheels. How will it work? It shakes to move the car (see Figure 6.6).

You can see the shake-drive action in a cell phone that is set to vibrate. Put the phone on a table with the ring set to vibrate and have someone call the number. The phone

Things you will need

- an adult
- notebook
- cardboard
- motor
- clip leads
- battery
- wheels
- axles (dowels)
- straws
- glue and tape

- plastic cable tie
- light weight, such as a coin
- extra dowels or a coat hanger
- wire cutters
- drill and bits
- block of wood (1 inch by 2 inches, 3 to 4 inches long)

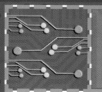
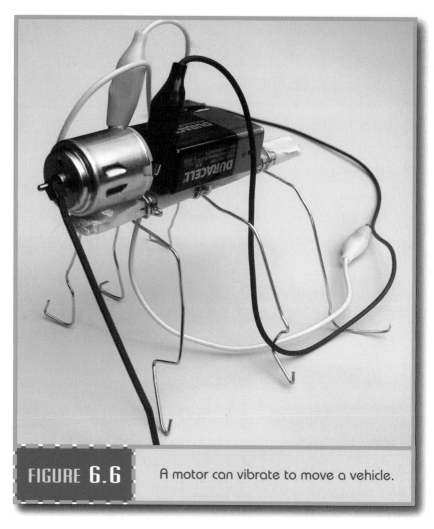

FIGURE **6.6**   A motor can vibrate to move a vehicle.

will jitter and may move across the table. What makes the phone vibrate?

Inside the phone is a tiny motor. On the shaft of the motor is a cam or eccentric weight. Rather than moving symmetrically around the motor shaft, the cam has more weight on one side than the other. Like a tire that is out of balance, the eccentric weight will throw the model around.

1. To add an off-center weight to a motor, use a small plastic cable tie. Put a few wraps of masking tape around the motor shaft and then install the tie, cinching it tightly over the masking tape. You can add a light weight to the end of the cable tie, such as a coin, but make sure you secure it well with glue and tape so that it won't fly off. Cut the tie so that it doesn't hit the ground when the motor spins.

2. Instead of using wheels, use stiff legs under a car body. Dowels that measure ⅛ inch or metal wire from a coat hanger work well. **With adult help,** drill holes in the bottom of a small piece of wood (1 inch by 2 inches, 3 to 4 inches long). Set equal-length legs of dowel or wire into the holes.

3. Mount the motor and battery on top.

4. Connect the wires and watch the jittering.

    Try changing the length of the legs, their position, and the direction they point. That is, the legs can be splayed to the sides or they can be pointed directly toward the floor.

    Try this jitter car on rigid surfaces, such as a concrete floor. Will that increase the motion? Does it work better with a longer or shorter cable tie?

Using Motors for Boats

As cool as cars are, boats can be even more fun. They can be a bit more difficult to build successfully, as you have to keep them from sinking. If you have a pond or pool available, experimenting with electric boats is great.

"Electric motors in boats? Are you nuts? You'll get shocked!" No, you won't get shocked if you use the batteries we suggest in this book. If you're not sure you can trust us, give a battery a test.

Safety note:

When doing experiments near water always keep alternating current electrical appliances far away. If an item has an electrical plug, do not use it near water.

The DC motors we recommend using in these experiments are robust and will operate when they are wet. However, immersion in salt water will ruin them quickly. Later, we will show how to protect the motors for use underwater.

Test a Battery

COOL!

A 9-volt or transistor battery has the highest voltage of any battery we suggest using. Wet one finger and place it across the two terminals of a fresh 9-volt battery. Can you feel anything?

Probably not. And, that's in direct contact with the battery terminals. Wetting your finger decreases the electrical resistance of your skin, so that electricity can flow more easily. Even then, you can't feel anything.

The point is that as long as you don't connect a bunch of batteries to get high voltages, you will be safe using batteries in boats. **NEVER use electricity from an outlet in or near water.**

Things you will need

- notebook
- 9-volt battery
- your finger

EXPERIMENT
7.2

COOL!

Swamp Boat

Have you seen or ridden in a swamp boat? These are flat-bottomed boats that skim across the shallow waters of swamps. They boats have gasoline engines that spin large propellers (safely enclosed in wire cages). You can make a model swamp boat.

You'll need the same materials you needed for the propeller car (Experiment 6.2), except you won't need wheels, straws, or dowels. But you will need a disposable cup for a motor mount. For a boat hull you can use a milk or juice carton, or you can make a hull out of plastic, wood, or other material. From the propeller car project you will need

Things you will need

- **notebook**
- **paper milk carton, or toy boat**
- **scissors, or knife and an adult**
- **motor**
- **battery**
- **clip leads**
- **propeller**
- **paper or plastic cup**
- **hot glue and tape**

a battery, clip leads, a motor, and propeller that fits the motor shaft (see Figure 7.1).

1. Paper half gallon milk cartons make great boat hulls. Cut one in half lengthwise with a sturdy pair of scissors, or have **an adult** help cut it with a knife. One carton can give two equal-sized hulls to experiment with.

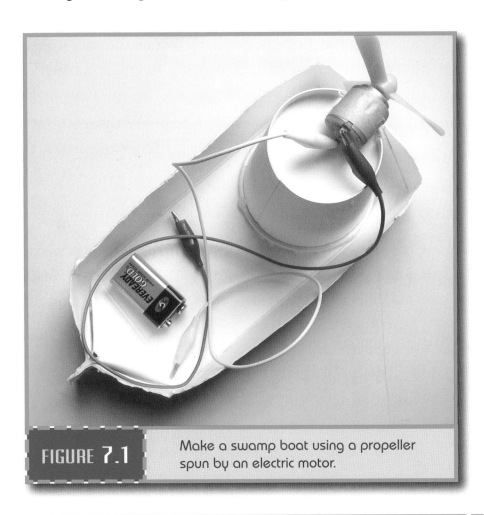

FIGURE 7.1   Make a swamp boat using a propeller spun by an electric motor.

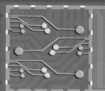
2. Mount the motor on the disposable cup. This is to get the propeller above the boat. You want the propeller to push air, not water.

3. Before gluing or taping the cup to the inside of the hull, test the positions of the motor mount (cup) and battery. Put the boat hull in a tub of water. Is the boat leaning to one side or to the front or back? Position the two heavy objects, the motor and battery, so that the boat is on an even keel. Then secure the motor mount and battery in position.

4. Connect the clip leads to the battery. Be careful not to let the spinning propeller hit your fingers because it will hurt.

5. Launch your swamp boat in a pond or pool. What happens? Most likely it will drive in circles. Try repositioning the motor to blow in the direction opposite to the way the boat is moving to correct the turn. That is, if the boat is going in circles to the right, reposition the motor so that it is pushing air slightly to the left. This will push the bow to the left.

6. You might need to also add a keel or sideboards. Cut flat pieces of a milk carton and tape them either to the bottom (for a keel) or sides (sideboards) of the boat. They should be pointing directly downward, to the bottom of the pool. Or try using a toy boat and mount

the motor, propeller, and battery in it, instead of using a milk carton for the hull.

6. Try reversing the leads to the battery. That is, make the boat go in the opposite direction by changing the direction the motor spins.

Once you have the boat working well, challenge your friends to a race. See who can make the fastest swamp boat.

Propellers

Most boats and ships use propellers in the water. If you are near large ships and see one that is riding high in the water (meaning it has no cargo), you might see the tips of the screw propellers breaking the water surface. If you do, notice how slowly the propeller is turning.

To make an in-water drive system (see Figure 7.2), you will want a slow-turning motor. You can use either a gear-head motor or try a less expensive motor powered by a single 1.5-volt cell.

Some science catalogs carry tiny boat propellers. These can work well, but the engineering challenge will be to fit

Things you will need

- notebook
- paper milk carton
- scissors
- motor or gear motor
- battery
- cocktail straws
- aluminum foil
- battery holder
- small nail or awl
- hot glue and tape
- clip leads
- propeller
- paper or plastic cup

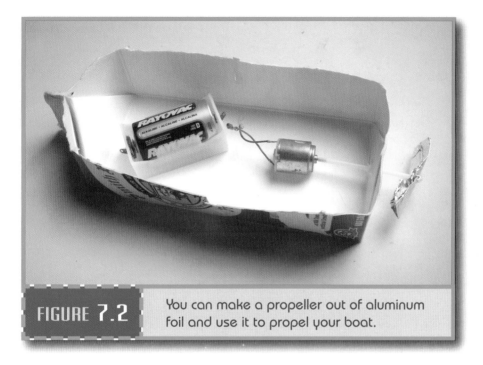

| FIGURE 7.2 | You can make a propeller out of aluminum foil and use it to propel your boat. |

them to a propeller shaft that attaches to the motor shaft. Tiny straws (cocktail straws) work well as propeller shafts.

1. You can make your own propeller. Fold a 1-inch by 2-inch piece of aluminum foil in half twice in both length and width. Press the folded foil firmly. Find the center of this aluminum rectangle and poke a small hole in it with a small nail or awl. Insert the propeller shaft through the hole and glue in place.

2. Propellers don't work if they are straight, so you need to bend the two blades. Hold the ends in each hand and twist each in opposite directions. Once the boat is

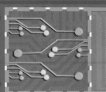

working, you can experiment with different amounts of twist to see what works best.

3. Use a half milk carton as in the previous experiment for a boat hull. Place the motor and propeller shaft in the boat to figure out where the motor should be located and at what angle the shaft will have to be for so that the propeller to be in the water.

4. Poke a hole through the back of the carton to fit the propeller shaft (cocktail straw) through from the outside.

5. Mount the motor on a disposable plastic or paper cup that you've cut to the right size and at the right angle. Glue the motor mount (cup) in place and glue the motor to the cup. Although hot glue will hold the motor reasonably well, you will be able to yank it off later if you want to use it for another project. Use just a dab of glue.

6. Slide the propeller shaft (straw) onto the motor shaft. If the propeller shaft doesn't fit snugly, wrap the motor shaft with a tiny piece of masking tape and then try again.

7. Because this propeller will need to turn slowly, use a single 1.5-volt battery. For an easy connection, use a battery holder. Use two clip leads to connect the battery to motor. Be prepared to be splashed!

8. These boats work well, but you have to engineer them to go in a straight line. Reposition the motor and propeller to point in the direction you want the bow to move.

If the boat turns to the right, angle the propeller toward the left side of the boat. This will tend to drive the bow (front) to the left, hopefully correcting the turn.

9. Try making other propellers. Instead of a two bladed propeller, try a four-bladed propeller. Make 2 two-bladed propellers and glue them onto the propeller shaft so that each blade is 90 degrees from the others. Most ships have four-bladed propellers. However, small boats usually have three-bladed propellers. Very slow trolling motors used for fishing in skiffs use two-bladed propellers. Submarine propellers can have 4, 5, or 7 blades.

Idea for a Science Fair Project

What in-water propeller design pushes the boat fastest? You can cut propellers out of disposable aluminum pie pans. Testing could be done for the amount of twist you apply to each blade, the number of blades, or the surface area of the propeller. To measure the surface area, weigh the propellers on a scientific scale at school. As long as each propeller is made of the same material, the weight will give an estimate for the relative size.

Side-Wheel Electric Boat

One way to transfer motion from a motor to an axle is with a belt. Using a rubber band as a belt, you can make a side-wheeler (see Figure 7.3). Side-wheel steam ships were in use in the nineteenth and early twentieth centuries. They carry two paddles amid ships.

1. You can make the paddles out of the same coated paper material that the boat hull is composed of. For each paddle, cut two squares out of a paper milk carton, notch each from the middle of one side into the center. Insert one notch into the other to make an X. You can

Things you will need

- notebook
- paper milk carton
- scissors
- motor
- battery
- battery holder
- clip leads

- propeller
- hole punch
- hot glue and tape
- pulley (optional)
- rubber band
- dowels

FIGURE 7.3 This side-paddle boat uses a rubber band to carry the motor's energy to the axle and the paddles.

strengthen the paddle by gluing pieces of straw or dowel between the intersecting blades of the paddle.

2. Cut a ¼-inch dowel about 4 inches wider than the milk carton hull. Use a hole punch to make evenly spaced holes on either side of the hull so that the paddles will push water backward and be out of the water during their forward movement.

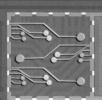
3. Pass the dowel through one of the holes in the hull, then loop several rubber bands onto the dowel. You will probably need only one rubber band, but the others are there in case the first one breaks.

4. Pass the dowel through the second side. Now glue the two paddles onto this axle. Put a generous amount of hot glue on the each end of the axle and hold it against the paddle between two of the blades.

5. This model works best with a slow motor. Use either a gearhead motor or a regular high-speed motor powered by a single 1.5-volt battery. Use a battery holder to make it easier to connect to a battery, unless it is a 9-volt battery.

6. To find where you should locate the motor, loop one rubber band onto the motor shaft (or pulley that is mounted on the motor shaft) and connect the motor to the battery. Pull the motor away from the axle until the rubber band has enough tension to make the paddles turn. When pushing water instead of air, the motor will have a much greater load and the belt will be more likely to slip, so pull the motor back a bit farther. Mark its position on the deck. If you are not using a pulley on the motor shaft, turn the motor slightly so that the motor shaft points away from the axle. This will help prevent the rubber band from riding off the shaft. Remove the rubber band from the motor shaft and glue the motor in place.

7. To help hold the motor against the pull of the rubber band, glue a short section of dowel in front of the motor. Hold the dowel against the motor and deck until the glue dries.

8. Test the boat in water to determine where to put the battery. You want the boat floating on an even keel. You don't want it leaning to one side or to be riding bow-down or stern-down. When you have found the right place for the battery, put a tiny dab of hot glue on the side of the battery or battery holder and hold it in place against the deck until the glue dries.

9. Connect the battery to the motor with clip leads and launch your boat. How well does it work?

   Could you add a second motor to the boat? You could either have it help drive the first axle or you could make a second axle. You could have one axle that has a paddle on one side only and the other axle on the other side. Then if you reverse the motor on one side, the boat will turn.

Idea for a Science Fair Project

If the paddles were larger, would the boat go faster? You could test three or more sizes of paddles and measure the speed of each. Graph the results to show how paddle size (or the number of paddles) affects the speed of the boat.

Hydraulic Drive

A pump consists of a motor and a device that moves water when it spins. There are many types of pumps. Some are designed to be submerged in water and others work best when kept dry. Check science catalogs for small pumps that run on batteries.

There are at least two ways to use a pump to propel a boat. The simplest way is to use vinyl tubing to carry the pumped water to the back of the boat. As the water is forced out of the tube, it will move the boat in the opposite direction. Flexible tubing gives you the option of steering the boat.

Things you will need

- notebook
- paper milk carton
- scissors
- pump (available through science catalogs)
- plastic tubing
- battery
- clip leads
- propeller
- paper or plastic cup

You could also store the energy of the pumped water in a plastic cup and use its weight to propel the boat. The pump picks water up from outside the boat and lifts it into the cup, which is centered on the hull. A straw or tube inserted into the side of the cup near the bottom allows the water to flow out of the cup and boat. As the water flows out of the straw, it moves the boat in the opposite direction.

1. Prepare a boat hull as you have in earlier projects.

2. Decide on a design for your pump-drive boat. If you will use the pump to fill a cup, mount the cup in the center of the hull. If you will have the pump push water out the back of the boat, make a hole in the boat to fit the flexible tubing.

3. Mount the pump and battery so that the boat can float on an even keel.

4. Attach clip leads and test your boat.

Waterproofing Motors

Using motors near water usually results in the motors getting wet. In freshwater this isn't much of a problem. Dry the outside of the motor and use a hair dryer to blow warm, dry air inside the motor.

If you will be using motors underwater or using them in water several times, consider waterproofing them. The methods we suggest here will make the motors safer, but won't guarantee that they will survive repeated dunkings.

1. Cover the vent holes in the motor casing. Use electrical tape that you can stretch over the holes. Cut the tape into small pieces that conform to the shape of the motor.

Things you will need

- **an adult**
- notebook
- motor
- candle wax
- electrical tape
- scissors
- petroleum jelly
- 35mm film canister
- nail and hammer
- matches
- soldering iron and solder

2. Use petroleum jelly or similar gel to help keep water from entering along the motor shaft. The deeper you place a motor in water, the more water pressure it experiences, and the more likely water will seep in. For shallow use or above-water use, however, the gel can keep water out.

3. If you plan to use the motors underwater, take one more step. Punch a small hole (for the motor shaft) in the end of a plastic 35mm film canister. A small nail and hammer will help you make the hole. After covering the cooling slots with electrical tape and greasing the motor shaft, slide the motor into the canister so that the shaft sticks out the hole. With the help of **an adult**, solder wires to both of the motor terminals so that you can connect it to a battery. With additional help of **an adult**, melt some liquid candle wax and pour this into the film canister. It helps to have some way of holding the canister erect while you are pouring and while the wax is hardening.

4. Test how well the waterproof motor works. Connect it to a battery and place the motor in some water. See how long it continues to spin.

CHAPTER 8

The Electric Factory

The models so far have been self-propelled. Here is a different approach to having fun with electric motors: make a gizmo that turns, spins, and moves, but is not a vehicle.

A simple electric factory can be made out of a small cardboard box. A shoe box is the right size. After making one or two of these models, you can get more creative with finding other materials to use. Look around for discarded toys or game pieces or even old appliances.

The idea is to use an electric motor to turn one or more driveshafts that move cams, cranks, gears, pulleys, and other devices in an interesting way. The best way to get started is to start building. Ideas will come to you as you build.

Build an Electric Sculpture

COOL!

1. Start with a sturdy cardboard box that can support an axle, motor, and other moving parts. Punch or drill holes in the center of each end to support an axle. To reduce the friction between the box and axle, insert short sections of a milkshake straw and glue these in place. Then insert a ¼-inch dowel through the two pieces of straw.

2. Decide how you will connect the motor to the axle. The easiest way is to use a belt drive with rubber bands (see Figure 8.1). You could also use gears or direct drive.

Things you will need

- notebook
- shoe box
- motors or gear motors
- battery
- cams, cranks, gears
- pulleys
- rubber bands
- clip leads
- scissors
- cardboard
- tape
- milkshake straws
- dowels
- hot glue
- drill and bits

FIGURE 8.1   Power your kinetic sculpture with a motor and connect it with a rubber band.

For the belt drive, put a rubber band on the axle, either inside the box or outside, and try driving the axle with a slow motor or a gearhead motor. Find the right tension and decide where to mount the motor. Mounting it inside the box has the advantage of giving you a solid platform to anchor the motor. However, with other mechanisms inside the box, it will get crowded. The belt will tend to slip more when you have added the other mechanisms, so position the motor so that the belt is tighter than it needs to be just to turn the axle.

3. Draw a center line along the length of the top of the box, directly above the axle. Make a hole along this line. If the box is made of light material, add a piece of thick cardboard or a thin piece of wood to help support the vertical axle that you will place in the hole.

4. Drill a hole in this piece and glue it directly above the hole in the box.

5. Make a push rod to go through the hole. Cut a circle out of cardboard and mount it on the end of a ¼-inch dowel. This will ride above a cam that you now place on the axle.

6. For the cam, cut a circle out of heavy cardboard, plastic, or wood and drill a hole off-center. Slide this cam onto the drive axle that's mounted in the box.

7. Insert the push rod from the inside of the box, out through the hole in the top of the box. Position the cam directly beneath the push rod and test the system. As you turn the drive axle by hand, it should rotate the cam and push the push rod up and down. You might need to glue the cam in place, but use only a tiny dab of glue because you will need to remove the cam from the axle if you want to add other components later.

What do you want the push rod to raise and lower? Do you have small toys to glue to the push rods? Can you make something out of cardboard and paper to attach?

8. When you've got all your components together, connect the clip leads to close the circuit and enjoy your kinetic sculpture.

American Science & Surplus
P.O. Box 1030
Skokie, IL 60076
888-724-7587
<http://www.sciplus.com>

KELVIN
280 Adams Blvd.
Farmingdale, NY 11735
800-535-8469
<http://www.kelvin.com>

Solarbotics Ltd.
3740D 11A Street NE
Suite #101
Calgary, AB T2E 6M6
Canada
866-276-2687
<http://www.solarbotics.com>

Glossary

ampere—A unit of electric current flow. It is often shortened to "amp."

bearing—A mechanical device that permits motion only in the desired direction. Bearings are used to stop unwanted motion in machines.

bushing—A cylindrical device that allows connections between two different-sized axles.

cam—A rotating wheel that moves a lever or rod. Rather than rotating around its center, some cams rotate around a point that is not in the center.

cam follower—A flat surface that rides on top of a cam and is attached to a rod (push rod) or lever.

commutator—An electric switch inside a motor that reverses the flow of electricity to change the direction of the electromagnets that keep the motor turning.

complete circuit—A series of electrical components that are connected so that electrons can flow from one terminal of a battery through all the components and back to the other terminal of the battery.

crank—A device for changing circular motion to back-and-forth motion (or the other way around). Cranks can be bent axles, or they can have parts perpendicular to the axle to provide leverage for turning the axle.

current—The flow of electrical charge. Current is measured in amps or amperes.

electric motor—A device that converts electrical energy into mechanical energy.

electromagnet—A magnet that depends on an electric current to generate its magnetic field.

gear—A toothed wheel. Gears are used to transmit energy.

gearhead motor—A motor that has a set of connected gears encased with it.

parallel circuit—An electrical circuit in which two or more components have the same voltage.

push rod—A rod used on a cam follower to transmit motion from a cam to another device.

series circuit—An electric circuit or connection in which the terminal of one device (motor, battery, lightbulb, etc.) is connected to a terminal of the adjacent device so that the entire group is connected from one to the other, end to end.

short circuit—A dangerous circuit in which an electric power source has its positive and negative terminals connected without any appreciable resistance in the connection.

switch—A device that opens or closes an electrical circuit.

torque—Rotational force. You exert torque when you turn something by using a lever. The longer the lever is, the more torque you can apply.

volt—A measure of the electrical force available. It is named for Italian scientist Alessandro Volta, who invented the battery.

Further Reading

Books

Carrow, Obert. *Put a Fan in Your Hat!: Inventions, Contraptions, and Gadgets Kids Can Build.* New York: McGraw-Hill, 1996.

Gabrielson, Curt. *Stomp Rockets, Catapults, and Kaleidoscopes: 30+ Amazing Science Projects You Can Build for Less than $1.* Chicago: Chicago Review Press, 2008.

Hammond, Richard. *Car Science.* New York: DK Children, 2008.

Parker, Steve. *Electricity.* New York: DK Children, 2005.

Somervill, Barbara. *Electrical Circuits and Currents.* Chicago: Raintree, 2009.

Suen, Anastasia. *Wired.* Watertown, Mass.: Charlesbridge, 2007.

Zubrowski, Bernie. *Blinkers and Buzzers.* Morrow Junior Books, 1991.

Internet Addresses

Internet resources for making a simple electric motor:

http://www.simplemotor.com/

http://www.evilmadscientist.com/article.php/
HomopolarMotor

http://motors.ceressoft.org/

Index